I0163065

GET CONNECTED

A Guide to the God Within

Stephenie L. Hardaway

Copyright © 2010 by Stephenie L. Hardaway

This book may not be reproduced in whole or in part or transmitted in any form, without written permission from the publisher.

ISBN 978-0-557-68386-4

This book is dedicated to my family and all those who are seeking the God within.

FOREWARD

I am not a scholar. I don't have a degree. I am an ordinary person on an extraordinary journey. I am just like you in that I am trying to make this life work the best I can. I have found that, for me, my best life involves God. I am a student. I love to read and dig into the meanings of what I read. I think I will always be a student. I love studying about different religions. From what I have studied so far, they seem to compliment rather than contradict one another. I do admit that I have a lot more studying to do.

I would implore each of you reading this to try studying different religions. Don't take anyone else's word for it. Explore for yourself and you will be amazed at what you find.

This book is written as an encourager to all of us seeking what we already have. Hopefully by the end you will be on your way to discovering who we all are on this beautiful planet.

INTRODUCTION

I was awakened at 6:30am by a voice telling me to get up and write. As I lay there, the words of this book (at least the start of it) were given to me. I was not feeling well, so I really did not want to get up. My thought was that I could do it later but the voice was insistent. So I got up and began to write.

We are all the sum parts of a whole. Everyone on this planet equals one. It has taken me quite a while to figure this out and yes, to even understand it. It is difficult to grasp sometimes because we are all taught to be individuals and see others as separate from ourselves. However, standing alone weakens us. Of course, there are times when it's necessary to stand alone. For example, Gandhi stood alone in his quest to bring peace. So did Martin Luther King Jr., Malcolm X, and not to mention Jesus the Christ. They stood alone in leadership. However, the one thing they taught was unity. A house divided against itself cannot stand.

In order to change our world we must be united. However, it seems that we find more reasons to separate than to come together. How do we get to this point of unity? The first step is to recognize who we are and whose we are. Once we recognize it, then we must be able to connect to it.

If you are truly seeking ways to improve your life individually and our lives as a whole then you must be open minded in your search. If you are truly seeking God then your mind must be open to understanding different viewpoints. Remember the sum total equals the whole.

God is pictured as the Father, the Creator of all that is. God is responsible for all life. Unity has an affirmation that states: I believe there is only one Presence and one Power active in my life now. What Presence? What Power? I say God. Others may use the terms Universe, Spirit or Source. It's all the same. Remember – open mind.

When I used to think of God, it was as a white man with a long white beard sitting on a throne watching us act crazy. It was impossible to measure up and that was okay according to how I was taught. We are not perfect and never will be so I shouldn't worry about it. But something in me felt that there had to be more to God. I have come a long way from that time in my life. The more I study, the closer I get to the real God. I truly understand what it means when it is said that we are children of God.

God is pictured in many ways. I choose to focus on the one that I continue to meet on a daily basis.

God the Father

My biological father was never in my life. I had a stepfather who did the best he knew how, but I never felt like I had a real dad. As I grew up seeing the fathers who did things with their children and encouraged their dreams, I felt cheated.

Even growing up going to church all of the time did not give me a sense of a personal God the Father. To me, God was like the rest of the fathers: a punisher, not there when you need them and gone if you mess up.

But I am thankful that I was blessed with an open mind. It's because of my open mind that I was able to study different religions and come to understand God the Father. Don't get me wrong. He's been there all along. I just had to find out for myself.

The dictionary defines father as the creator of, to take responsibility of, protector, provider and source. These are all attributes of God.

God is the Creator. We were given a perfect world in which to live. It has everything we all need to live comfortably. It is our greed, among many other things that has contributed to the growing pain our planet suffers. God took responsibility for us before ever creating us. The planet is full of plants that have medicinal qualities. There are precious stones on certain continents that can provide a good living for the people that live there. There is food all around. There really is no excuse for starvation.

God is our protector. Just read Psalm 91 and you will know that there is nothing God won't do for you. As our human fathers should protect us, God the Father does.

God is the source for all we need. There is no other. God is peace, joy, love, protection and abundance all in one.

We must take God out of the box that religion has created. How can you box Spirit? God is not man who is limited in thoughts and actions. God is limitless and nothing can hold Him (pronoun used for simplicity). God is always there; ready and available. He has always been and always will be. He is the beginning and the end. In Revelation he repeatedly says, "I am the Alpha and Omega, the Beginning and the End." God is it! So why is it so hard for us to really know God?

Jesus – The Son

I grew up with Jesus as my big brother. He was the one who God sent and who came willingly to be killed for me. How lucky was I? Someone would die for me!

Again, growing older shined a whole new light on Jesus. No longer was the crucifixion the main focus for me. The main focus became Jesus himself.

I love Jesus. His character is so understandable. He recognized about himself what we fail to believe about ourselves. There is God in each of us. Jesus was definitely on a different plane than those around Him, but the amazing thing is that some of those, whose faith was strong enough, began to do what Jesus had done.

In the book of Acts, Peter raised a woman from the dead just as Jesus had raised Lazarus. In John 10:10, Jesus said that He came that they may have life, and have it more abundantly. Jesus was a walking, talking fully realized representative of God. What do I mean by fully realized? I mean He knew who God was and who He was in relation to God. He was able to do things that others could not. Why? Because of His connection with God.

Many people say that Jesus was already God; therefore it's not possible for us to be like Him. I say this is possible. The Bible says nothing is impossible with God. Jesus did the one thing that so many of us do not. He kept himself connected to God. He fasted forty days and forty nights in the wilderness. He would often get away from everyone to pray. He spent time in the silence with God. In all Jesus did, He acknowledged the Father. He said when you see me you've seen the Father. In John 14 it is clear that Jesus was following the Father's instructions. The words He spoke came directly from the Source.

What I'm saying is this. We all come from the same Source. So again I ask, "Why is it so hard for us to really know God?"

Us - The Children of God

I was taught that as a child of God, I had to be obedient, respect my elders, keep the Sabbath day holy and treat others as I want to be treated. However, as I grew older and became curious about the God I'm supposed to serve, I learned more about Him and myself than I thought possible.

I am a CHILD OF GOD! It was such a wonderful feeling when I FINALLY realized what that meant! I had let people tell me what it meant for so long that I did not think God could ever love me.

One particular day changed all of that. I was in a corner in my bedroom crying my eyes out and feeling like I wanted to die. I felt very unloved and unlovable. But I heard a voice as clear as day say, "Stephenie, you are my child and I love you." From that day - no matter what – I would not let anyone tell me that God did not and does not love me. My journey since has been to maintain my connection and get as close to God as possible.

I realized that we all come from God which truly makes us His children. There is a piece of God in each of us. Some have chosen to try and bring that piece closer to the surface so that they can live an abundant life in every way. Some choose to use it when necessary, some choose to ignore it altogether and some have forgotten that it's there. Make no doubt about it, it is there!

Jesus came, not just to die, but to show us how to live here as a reflection of God. When you look at the life He lived as shown in the Bible, it's clear that He was a man as well as God. He ate, slept, worked, prayed, studied and connected. His connection was very strong because that's what He focused on. He knew that with God anything could be done. He knew that yearning for yesterday or tomorrow would not help you today.

These are lessons that we must learn if we are ever to operate in the power of God. There comes a time when we must prepare ourselves for our role in this life. Just as royalty prepares the next generation to take their place, so does God want to prepare us.

That spark of God-ness that is in every one of us attempts to move us toward the direction we are supposed to go. However, we must cooperate. If we truly want peace that passes all understanding – we must connect. If we want to experience true unconditional love – we must connect. If we want to live the abundant life that has been promised, but so few have obtained, then we must connect.

We are children of God with all the rights and privileges that come with our birthright. Our Father is limitless, infinite and exists within us. But it is up to us to realize that He has always been there. All we have to do is connect.

How do we connect? There are different ways for different people. The ways I currently experience God is through music and silence. God speaks to me when I speak to Him and when I truly listen. You can also recognize when others are being used to speak something into you but this requires attention. Not everyone who speaks over you is speaking for God.

Time is out for letting everyone else tell us what to believe! We must study so that we can experience God ourselves and therefore eliminate the chances of us being hoodwinked and hurt by those who misuse and misrepresent God. Remember He is our Father and is available to all but you must connect.

God – The Source

Take God at His word. Believe what He says. He has never left us. All that we seek to fulfill us, He is. Drugs and alcohol are bandages for the deeper wounds caused by self-separation. When we decide that we can make it on our own then we have chosen to separate ourselves from God. There is nothing that we need that God cannot provide. After all; if the earth is the Lord's and the fullness thereof, why look elsewhere? When Joshua took over for Moses God gave him the same promise that He gave Moses. In Deuteronomy 31:6, He told Joshua that He would never fail him or forsake him.

It's the same for us. God does not leave us. He lives in each of us, yet we constantly look outside of ourselves for what we need. I speak not only of material things but also emotional support. We so often are pulled by life's challenges that we forget the strength of God lies within us. We only need to recognize it and pull from it. Read Psalm 91 sometimes and picture the words as you read them. You will see the picture of strength that God provides.

One thing Jesus spoke about was not worrying about tomorrow. In Matthew 6:25 – 34 Jesus gives examples of birds that do not worry about anything. They are NOW MINDED. All they care about is NOW. They don't worry about what to eat, wear or where they will sleep. They know that food is there. They know that the trees are there for them to make their homes. Jesus said in verse 26, "Behold the fowls of the air; for they sow not, neither do they reap, nor gather into barns; yet your heavenly Father feedeth them. Are ye not much better than they?" Well, are you? Basically, Jesus was saying that all we need has already been provided. It is up to us to accept it.

This idea has proven to be difficult for many to accept. We have the tendency to see God with our finite eyes, yet Jesus said that God is spirit and they that worship Him must worship Him in Spirit and truth. What is that saying? We cannot go to God in our humanness and expect to understand how He works. Only spirit can understand spirit.

God is available now. He is available at the time we need Him. There is nothing outside of us that provides the peace that God does. Philippians 4:7 speaks of peace that passes all understanding. This is a peace that most don't believe is available and guess what…for them it is not! How can you accept something you think does not exist? Until we really get in touch with our real, personal Father, Creator, God; we will forever struggle. Once you are tired of the struggle and find that nothing outside works you will have no choice. You will either look to the God that was always there or cease living.

Life without God is not life. It is walking on a tightrope with no safety net. That is no way to live and we were not created to exist. We were created to enjoy life. Jesus said that he came that we may have and enjoy life and have it in abundance. How wonderful is that? He came to show us that it's possible to live here and really enjoy the abundance of God.

How often have you looked around at this wonderful place we call home? How beautiful is this planet that was given to us? I was a person who was not into nature at all. My mother on the other hand probably has hundreds of pictures of trees taken during autumn. She loves when they change colors. When I began my search in earnest I would force myself to slow down and look at the trees. Now I notice them when I am driving or riding. I love looking at mountains. My dream is to drive cross country with my family and stop along the way just to look at the scenery. I can see it in my mind as I type this and I know that we will be able to take the trip soon.

This is what I mean when I say that God is available and abundance is everywhere. I don't know how we are going to take the trip but I rest in assurance that it is done. I wish that for everyone.

The Art of the Connection

You're probably thinking, "How do I know if I am connected to God?" The easiest way to tell is by looking at your life. I'm not talking about how much stuff you have but your life overall. Jesus said, "I am the true vine and you are the branches. You will know a tree by the fruit it bears." So how is your life? Are you in chaos or misery? Are you speeding through life? Or have you found the sweet spot? That's where everything may not be perfect but you are truly ok.

Everyday is not going to be a picnic. But hey, you are no longer looking at the circumstances. You now keep your eyes on the Source. You don't look for the outside world to take care of you or your issues. You now recognize the bigness of God. He is bigger than anything we have to face. When things seem impossible, you know that nothing is impossible with God. In John 3:1-2 Nicodemus tells Jesus that they knew He came from God. Why? The answer is simple. No one could do what He did without being connected.

When I think or speak about God, my body tingles. I can't be still. The awesomeness of God is overwhelming and at the same time humbling. To think that He is available to anyone at anytime and all we have to do is activate our connection. What I am saying is:

PLUG IN

Work With God – Not Against Him

So often you hear about faith. Jesus said if you have faith the size of a mustard seed, you could tell the mountain to be removed and it would. Don't laugh, but I once thought that Jesus was speaking of a literal mountain. Now, I know that He was speaking of obstacles in our lives. There are mountains of poverty, mountains of illness, mountains of judgment, unforgiveness, etc. Anything that keeps you from growing and prospering is a mountain.

How do we get those mountains to move? We do so by acknowledging the mountains and opening ourselves to receive God's guidance in dealing with them. Some of us try to tackle the mountains ourselves which prevents God from working things out. For example, I know there are people who are barely making it financially. They decide to take things in their own hands and that's when mistakes are made. We bet on the lottery, casinos and some even bet on drugs to get them out of poverty. God has placed in every person some idea, gift or talent that can be used to provide a great living.

I had a terrible time deciding what talent I really wanted to hone in on. I never really thought of myself as particularly talented. I looked at my talents as just things that I liked to do. I love to bake and have received quite a few compliments on my baked goods. Although people would tell me that I should have a bakery; it took awhile before I could visualize it myself. I realized that I could use my love of baking to make a good living. Once that decision had been made, it seemed as if things had fallen into place. I received an email from a school that had the baking program I wanted. I was excited speaking with the admissions representative. Everything just felt so right and the tour of the school seemed to cement my belief that I belonged there. Then I ran into the money issue. After speaking with the assistant director of admissions, I knew that it would cost more money than I had. It was during this time that I started reading Napoleon Hill's book "Think & Grow Rich." I was also reading Eckhart Tolle's "Power of Now" and Wayne Dyer's "The Power of Intention."

These books in conjunction with listening to Rev. Della Reese-Lett and Rev. Chris Michaels helped to put me on the path to fulfilling my purpose. The morning God woke me to write this book was when I finally realized that I have all I need within me. It is available to me just as yours is available to you. All we have to do is open up and accept it. That is what I have done.

Be Still

Earlier I spoke of finding God in the stillness. You find in Psalms 46:10, God says be still and know that He is God. That says it all. Stillness is a requirement in knowing God. It is very difficult to hear God when so many things demand our attention. Therefore, it is up to us to make the time in our busy lives for God. Stillness takes some getting us to. You will find the famous "monkey chatter" constantly goes on in your mind. It can be frustrating if you let it. It was for me in the beginning. I would try to fight it and when it didn't stop I would give up. However, I wanted to have that time with God, so I kept trying different methods.

I began to listen to music at the beginning of my meditation. The kind of music that would, as I call it, get my mind right. Once my mind was focused on the words that I was singing, I would turn the music off and God was right there. The Presence was filling the room. I was ecstatic! I don't know how long it lasted but by the time it was over I was a blubbering but happy mess. I began speaking to God all day and I knew that He was listening. I have no doubts.

His presence has made me conscious of my behavior, language, attitude and thoughts. There are times when I mess up but I ask for forgiveness and move on. I have also included affirmations in my daily life. They are a great tool to keep me focused.

In Revelation 3:20, Jesus said "Behold, I stand at the door and knock; if any man hear my voice and open the door, I will come in to him and will sup with him and he with me." This verse lets us know that He waits for us to invite Him in. Once we do we must be ready for what follows. Conversation. Not us just talking to Him but listening as well. He is not rude or forceful. He wants to be invited and until we do, He waits faithfully. All it takes is for us to open up and say hello.

My question to you is, "Are you ready for your life to change?" Because it will. Once you acknowledge God's presence in your life and spend quality time with Him you will notice changes. Some may be small, some large, but there will be changes. Life just gets better because you are aware of the power within you. There are life experiences that you will have but you no longer rely on yourself. Your first thought becomes "God, how do I handle this situation?" Sometimes it can be, "God, how do I wait on YOU to handle this situation?" Waiting can be difficult, if you don't know how to wait.

You don't stop living. You become more aware of people and things because you never know how the answer will come. The answer does come but you must be able to recognize it. Before I really developed an actual relationship with God, I allowed other things to distract me. I focused on the circumstances instead of the circumstance changer. I'm not saying you have to fool yourself. I am saying don't dwell on the negative because it will take over your life. My life is not perfect. Neither is it the stress-mess where I once dwelled. The changes have come swiftly at times and very slowly at others. However, I am now able to rest in the assurance that God has my back. As James said, "Faith without works is dead." I do my part and know that God is doing His. With that assurance, it becomes easier to wait.

I know that my desires were given to me by God. They are there so that I can live the life God has for me. When you know what you want – really know – then it's time to move. Desire pushes you to achievement. I have many desires and they push me to find ways to use the gifts I have been given in order to achieve them. It sounds funny but your desires push you to fulfill your desires.

The Beginning of Connection is Seeking God

Hebrews 11:6 says "But without faith it is impossible to please him; for he that cometh to God must believe that he is and that he is a rewarder of them that diligently seek him." I choose to end this book with the way our connection should begin. It starts with FAITH! In order to have a relationship with God you have to know that He is there. There must be a certainty within you about God. How can you have a relationship with one you don't believe exists?

There are those who believe that He exists but don't believe He will do what He said. There are also those who believe that He will do it, but not for them. Finally, there are those who don't believe that God is actually living within them and will work through them to give them the life they desire.

The verse says when we come to God we must believe. Lack of belief is what keeps you stuck. Again, you cannot expect anything if there is no FAITH! I often wondered why many faithful churchgoers' lives never seemed to change or improve. Why did they come up for prayer every Sunday? It is good when the faithful pray for you, but remember you must also pray yourself. It is a necessity to spend time with God. I found that so many of us are more faithful to the church building than to God. In realizing that my God is bigger than anything I face, I was able to move beyond just being faithful to the building. I did not want to testify about the devil and his antics. I knew that we should talk about God and what HE was doing in our lives. I knew then that I was on a different page and wanted more. God is all powerful, but until you acknowledge that, back up and give Him reign over your life, nothing changes.

The final sentence of the scripture says that God is a rewarder of those who diligently seek Him. Diligently is defined by Merriam-Webster dictionary as characterized by steady, earnest, and energetic effort. It also says PAINSTAKING. What does that mean? It means that it's an everyday walk that takes effort. It is not always easy and may take longer than we want. It's not something that you can do one day, skip a few days, come back and be on the same wavelength as before. This is not to say that God won't be there when you get back. But you lose time in developing the relationship and getting stronger in your belief. It's a steady walk.

Once you develop that ongoing relationship with God, the reward is unbelievable. Your reward is having the almighty, all powerful, omniscient, omnipresent, Alpha & Omega on your side. That means that no matter what comes your way, you are not alone to face it. You have the God of Psalms 18:2; 19:14 & 27:1 – the God of Strength. You have the God of 2 Corinthians 9:8 – the God of Abundance. You have the God of 1 John 4:8 – the God of Love. Finally you have the God of Philippians 4:7 – the God of Peace.

It's no wonder that life becomes sweeter when God rewards you with the knowledge that He will never leave you nor forsake you. All other things are nothing in comparison. What you do with your reward is up to you.

Yes it's true that with God's help we can manifest our desires. But this book is about more than that. This is about enriching your WHOLE life. For those who have difficulty believing that it's possible to have a real relationship with God I suggest you try it. Take a week out of your life and get alone with God everyday. Start with 5 minutes of quiet time. Let the monkey chatter go on. Do not fight it or you will be distracted to the point of giving up. Once you learn to move beyond the mind talk it becomes easier to rest in the stillness. Remember that God told us, "BE STILL AND KNOW THAT I AM GOD."

www.ingramcontent.com/pod-product-compliance
Lightning Source LLC
Chambersburg PA
CBHW060101050426
42448CB00011B/2570